Soprano Volume 2
Revised Edition

THE SINGERS MUSICAL THEATRE ANTHOLOGY

A collection of songs from the musical stage, categorized by voice type. The selections are presented in their authentic settings, excerpted from the original vocal scores.

ISBN 978-0-7935-3050-2

HAL•LEONARD®
CORPORATION

7777 W. BLUEMOUND RD. P.O. BOX 13819 MILWAUKEE, WI 53213

Visit Hal Leonard Online at
www.halleonard.com

Foreword

It is apparent to me that the most important and lasting body of performable American music for singers has come from the musical theatre and musical film. The classical tradition as it had been continued in the United States has produced few major composers who have written extensively for the voice, composing a relatively small body of sometimes profound and beautiful literature, but often relevant only to specialized audiences.

In pre-rock era popular traditions, the songs that were not written for the stage or film are largely inferior in quality to those written for Broadway and Hollywood (although there are plenty of exceptions to this general rule). Perhaps the reason is simply that the top talent was attracted and nurtured by those two venues, and inspired by the best performers. But it's also possible that writing for a character playing some sort of scene, no matter how thin the dramatic context (sometimes undetectable), has inherently produced better songs. Compare a Rodgers and Hart ballad from the 1930s (which are all from musicals) to just an average pop ballad from that time not from the stage or screen, if you can dig one up, and you might see what I mean. Popular music of the rock era, primarily performers writing dance music for themselves to record, is almost a completely different aesthetic, and is most often ungratifying for the average singer to present in a typical performance with piano accompaniment.

The five volumes that comprise the original edition of *The Singer's Musical Theatre Anthology*, released in 1986, contain many of the most famous songs for a voice type, as well as being peppered with some more unusual choices. Volume Two of the series allows a deeper investigation into the available literature. This revised edition (2000) adds some significant songs. I have attempted to include a wide range of music, appealing to many different tastes and musical and vocal needs. As in the first volumes, whenever possible the songs are presented in what is their most authentic setting, excerpted from the vocal score or piano/rehearsal score, in the key originally performed and with the original piano accompaniment arrangement (which is really a representation of the orchestra, of course, although Kurt Weill was practically the only Broadway composer to orchestrate his own shows). A student of this subject will notice that these accompaniments are quite a bit different from the standard sheet music arrangements that were published of many of these songs, where the melody is put into a simplified piano part and moved into a convenient and easy piano key, without much regard to vocal range.

In the mezzo-soprano/belter volumes, I have restricted the choices to songs for a belting range, although they don't necessarily need to be belted, and put any songs sung in what theatre people call "head voice" or "soprano voice" in the soprano volumes. Classically trained mezzo-sopranos will be comfortable with many of the songs in the soprano books.

The "original" keys are presented here, although that often means only the most comfortable key for the original performer. Transpositions for this music are perfectly acceptable. Some songs in these volumes might be successfully sung by any voice type. Classical singers and teachers using these books should remember that the soprano tessitura of this style of material, which often seems very low, was a deliberate aesthetic choice, aimed at clarity of diction, often done to avoid a cultured sound in a singing voice inappropriate to the desired character of the song and role, keeping what I term a Broadway ingenue range. Barbara Cook and Julie Andrews are famous examples of this kind of soprano, with singing concentrated in an expressive and strong middle voice.

Richard Walters, editor
May, 2000

THE SINGER'S MUSICAL THEATRE ANTHOLOGY

Soprano Volume 2

Revised Edition

Contents

ABOUT THE SHOWS

ALLEGRO

MUSIC: Richard Rodgers
LYRICS AND BOOK: Oscar Hammerstein II
DIRECTOR AND CHOREOGRAPHER: Agnes de Mille
OPENED: 10/10/47, New York; a run of 315 performances

The third Rodgers and Hammerstein Broadway musical, *Allegro* was their first with a story that had not been based on a previous source. It was a particularly ambitious undertaking, with a theme dealing with the corrupting effect of big institutions on the young and idealistic. The saga is told through the life of a doctor, Joseph Taylor Jr., from his birth in a small midwestern town to his 35th year. We follow Joe's progress as he grows up, goes to school, marries a local belle, joins the staff of a large Chicago hospital that panders to wealthy hypochondriacs, discovers that his wife is unfaithful, and, in the end, returns to his home town with his adoring nurse, Emily, to rededicate his life to healing the sick and helping the needy. The show's innovations included a Greek chorus to comment on the action both to the actors and the audience, and the use of multi-level performing areas with abstract sets. "So Far" is sung by Beulah, Joe's flirtatious and temporary girlfriend. (It's another example of a Hammerstein love song between two people who haven't begun a relationship.)

ANYTHING GOES

MUSIC AND LYRICS: Cole Porter
BOOK: Guy Bolton and P.G. Wodehouse, Howard Lindsay and Russel Crouse
DIRECTOR: Howard Lindsay
CHOREOGRAPHER: Robert Alton
OPENED: 11/21/34, New York; a run of 420 performances

Cole Porter's best score of the 1930s is a fun-filled story taking place on an ocean liner about a group of oddball characters, including a nightclub singer, an enamoured stowaway, a debutante, and an underworld criminal disguised as a clergyman. Featuring a fresh, young Ethel Merman, the show was one of the biggest hits of its time, containing such hits as the title song, "You're the Top," "I Get a Kick Out of You," "Blow, Gabriel, Blow," and "All Through the Night." *Anything Goes* played Off Broadway in a 1962 production (239 performances), and enjoyed its biggest success in a 1987 Broadway revival starring Patti LuPone (804 performances). There is a 1936 filmed version, and another movie from 1956 with the title *Anything Goes*, but which bears little resemblance to the original. An excellent new recording, faithful to the 1934 original production, was released in the 1980s featuring Frederica Von Stade, Cris Groenendaal, and Kim Griswell.

CONVERSATION PIECE

MUSIC, LYRICS AND BOOK: Noël Coward
DIRECTOR: Noël Coward
OPENED: 1/15/34, London; a run of 177 performances
             10/23/34, New York; a run of 55 performances

In *Conversation Piece*, theatregoers were transported back to the fashionable seaside resort of Brighton during the Regency period in England. The stylish operetta was concerned with an impoverished French duke and his attempts to find a suitably wealthy husband for his ward, though eventually the two follow their secret hearts and confess their love for each other. The musical was written expressly for Yvonne Printemps (she sang "I'll Follow My Secret Heart") by the multi-talented Noël Coward, who also played the part of the duke when *Conversation Piece* first opened in London. Most of the original cast was recruited for the New York engagement, except for the substitution of Pierre Fresnay for Mr. Coward.

THE ENCHANTRESS

MUSIC: Victor Herbert
LYRICS AND BOOK: Harry B. Smith
OPENED: 10/9/11, Washington, D.C.
             12/11, New York

The Irish born Victor Herbert (1859-1924) was the most successful American composer of his time. He and his mother moved to Germany in 1866 when she married a German physician, and he received his musical training in that country, becoming an excellent cellist. Herbert's wife, a soprano, was engaged by the Metropolitan Opera, and he came along to New York, soon to be at the center of the city's musical life as a cellist and conductor. He began composing operettas in 1894 and wrote 40 such works in the next 30 years. The plots of these pieces are formulaic and often negligible. The only one performed regularly is *Babes in Toyland* (1903), although *The Red Mill* (1906) was successfully revived on Broadway in 1945 and was Herbert's biggest hit in his time.

The material in this section is by Stanley Green and Richard Walters, some of which was previously published elsewhere.

EVENING PRIMROSE

MUSIC AND LYRICS: Stephen Sondheim
TELEPLAY: James Goldman
DIRECTOR: Paul Bogart
TELECAST: 11/16/66

The short-lived ABC series *Stage 67* presented original teleplays, mostly by theatre writers in New York. Based on a John Collier story, *Evening Primrose* is about a poet who hides out in a department store to get away from the world. Much to his surprise, he meets hermits who have been hiding in there for years, and among them is a girl—they fall in love. Most of the music from this show was recorded by Bernadette Peters and Mandy Patinkin on his "Dress Casual" album.

EVITA

MUSIC: Andrew Lloyd Webber
LYRICS: Tim Rice
DIRECTOR: Harold Prince
CHOREOGRAPHER: Larry Fuller
OPENED: 6/23/78, London; a run of 2,900 performances
　　　　　9/25/79, New York; a run of 1,567 performances

Because of its great success in London, *Evita* was practically a pre-sold hit when it began its run on Broadway. Based on the events in the life of Argentina's strong-willed leader, Eva Peron, the musical—with Patti LuPone in the title role in New York—traced her rise from struggling actress to wife of dictator Juan Peron (Bob Gunton), and virtual co-ruler of the country. Part of the concept of the show is to have a slightly misplaced Che Guevera (played by Mandy Patinkin) as a narrator and conscience to the story of Eva's quick, greedy rise to power and her early death from cancer. "Another Suitcase in Another Hall" is a poignant "bimbo" song, sung by Juan Peron's previous and temporary co-habitant upon being kicked out on the street, replaced by Eva.

FIORELLO!

MUSIC: Jerry Bock
LYRICS: Sheldon Harnick
BOOK: Jerome Weidman and George Abbott
DIRECTOR: George Abbott
CHOREOGRAPHER: Peter Gennaro
OPENED: 11/23/59, New York; a run of 795 performances

New York's favorite mayor, Fiorello LaGuardia, was a peppery, pugnacious reformer whose larger-than-life personality readily lent itself to depiction on the musical stage. With Tom Bosley making an auspicious Broadway debut in the title role, *Fiorello!* covered the ten year period in LaGuardia's life before he became mayor. It begins with his surprise election to congress prior to World War I, and "When Did I Fall in Love" is sung by his adoring wife after he strides off to work at Capitol Hill. *Fiorello!* had the distinction of being the third musical to win the Pulitzer Prize in Drama, joining the ranks of *Of Thee I Sing* and *South Pacific*.

GUYS AND DOLLS

MUSIC AND LYRICS: Frank Loesser
BOOK: Abe Burrows and Jo Swerling
DIRECTOR: George S. Kaufman
CHOREOGRAPHER: Michael Kidd
OPENED: 11/24/50, New York; a run of 1,200 performances

Populated by the hard-shelled but soft-centered characters who inhabit the world of writer Damon Runyon, this "Musical Fable of Broadway" tells the tale of how Miss Sarah Brown of the Save-a-Soul Mission saves the souls of assorted Times Square riff-raff while losing her heart to the smooth-talking gambler, Sky Masterson. "I'll Know" is sung as a duet by Sarah and Sky early in their acquaintance. "If I Were a Bell" shows Sarah under the unfamiliar and, for the moment, giddy effects of alcohol supplied by Sky. An enormously successful revival opened on Broadway in 1992. The 1955 film version stars Frank Sinatra, Marlon Brando, Jean Simmons and Vivian Blaine.

JACQUES BREL IS ALIVE AND WELL AND LIVING IN PARIS

MUSIC: Jacques Brel
LYRICS: Jacques Brel, others (in French); English lyrics by Eric Blau, Mort Schumann
OPENED: 1968, New York

A long running intimate Off Broadway hit, the revue is a collection of some 25 songs by French songwriter Jacques Brel (he wrote both music and lyrics for some, lyrics only for others). The show is conceived for 4 players (2 men, 2 women), and the songs are full of contrasts in subject matter, from the draft, to old age, to bullfights, to death, to love. A film version was released in 1975. Brel (1929-1978) became a cabaret star in Paris only after no one else would perform his material.

THE KING AND I

MUSIC: Richard Rodgers
LYRICS AND BOOK: Oscar Hammerstein II
DIRECTOR: John van Bruten
CHOREOGRAHER: Jerome Robbins
OPENED: 3/29/51, New York; a run of 1,246 performances

The idea of turning Margaret Landon's novel *Anna and the King of Siam* into a musical first occurred to Gertrude Lawrence, who saw it as a suitable vehicle for her return to the Broadway musical stage. Based on the diaries of an adventurous Englishwoman, the story is set in Bangkok in the early 1860s. Anna Leonowens, who has accepted the post of schoolteacher to the Siamese king's children, has frequent clashes with the monarch but eventually comes to exert great influence on him, particularly in creating a more democratic society for his people. The show marked the fifth collaboration between Richard Rodgers and Oscar Hammerstein II, and their third to run over one thousand performances.

Cast opposite Miss Lawrence (who died in 1952 during the run of the play) was the then little known Yul Brynner. In 1956 he co-starred with Deborah Kerr in the movie version. In 1992 a new recording starring Julie Andrews and Ben Kingsley was released to mixed reviews. "I Whistle a Happy Tune" is sung at the top of the show by Anna and her young son as a bit of reassurance in arriving alone in a strange land.

KISMET

MUSIC AND LYRICS: Robert Wright and George Forrest, based on Alexander Borodin
BOOK: Charles Lederer and Luther Davis
DIRECTOR: Albert Marre
CHOREOGRAPHER: Jack Cole
OPENED: 12/3/53, New York; a run of 583 performances

The story of *Kismet* was adapted from Edward Knoblock's play first presented in New York in 1911 as a vehicle for Otis Skinner. The music of *Kismet* was adapted from themes by Alexander Borodin, from such works as the "Polovetzian Dances" and "In the Steppes of Central Asia." The musical's action occurs within a twenty-four hour period from dawn to dawn, in and around ancient Baghdad, where a Public Poet (first played by Alfred Drake), assumes the identity of Jauu the beggar and gets into all sorts of Arabian Nights adventures. At the end of the day, he is elevated to the position of Emir of Baghdad. His daughter, Marsinah, sings "And This Is My Beloved" to the young Prince Caliph, her new husband. The film version was made by MGM in 1955. A new recording of the musical was released in 1992 with opera star Samuel Ramey in the role of the poet and soprano Ruth Ann Swensen as Marsinah.

KISS ME, KATE

MUSIC AND LYRICS: Cole Porter
BOOK: Samuel and Bella Spewack
DIRECTOR: John C. Wilson
CHOREOGRAPHER: Hanya Holm
OPENED: 12/30/48, New York; a run of 1,077 performances

The genesis of Cole Porter's longest running musical occurred in 1935 when producer Saint Subber, then a stagehand for the Theatre Guild's production of Shakespeare's *The Taming of the Shrew*, became aware that its stars, Alfred Lunt and Lynn Fontanne, quarreled almost as much in private as did the characters in the play. Years later he offered this parallel story as the basis for a musical comedy to the same writing trio, Porter and the Spewacks, who had already worked on the successful show *Leave It to Me!* The entire action of *Kiss Me, Kate* occurs backstage and onstage at Ford's Theatre, Baltimore, during a tryout of a musical version of *The Taming of the Shrew*. The main plot concerns the egotistical actor-producer Fred Graham and his temperamental ex-wife Lili Vanessi who—like Shakespeare's Petruchio and Kate—fight and make up and eventually demonstrate their enduring affection for each other. One of the chief features of the score is the skillful way Cole Porter combined his own musical world (songs like "So in Love," "Too Darn Hot," "Why Can't You Behave?") with a Shakespearean world (songs like "I Hate Men"). Lilli Vanessi sings "I Hate Men" when playing the shrew character, Kate.

LITTLE MARY SUNSHINE

MUSIC, LYRICS AND BOOK: Rick Besoyan
DIRECTORS: Ray Harrison and Rick Besoyan
CHOREOGRAPHER: Ray Harrison
OPENED: 11/18/59, New York (Off Broadway); a run of 1,143 performances

Little Mary Sunshine, a witty, melodious takeoff of the *Naughty Marietta/Rose-Marie*/Jeannette MacDonald-Nelson Eddy school of operetta, was initially presented at a nightclub some three years before the long-running production opened Off Broadway. The story is set in the Colorado Rockies early in the century, and deals with the romance between the mincing heroine and stalwart Captain Big Jim Warrington, who saves his beloved from the clutches of a treacherous Indian just in time for their "Colorado Love Call" duet. "Look for a Sky of Blue" is Mary's entrance number in the show, sung with a pack of admiring but gentlemanly forest rangers.

A LITTLE NIGHT MUSIC

MUSIC AND LYRICS: Stephen Sondheim
BOOK: Hugh Wheeler
DIRECTOR: Harold Prince
CHOREOGRAPHER: Patricia Birch
OPENED: 2/25/73, New York; a run of 601 performances

Based on Ingmar Bergman's 1955 film, *Smiles of a Summer Night*, the score for *A Little Night Music* is composed in 3 (3⁄4, 3⁄8, 9⁄8, etc.), and contains Sondheim's biggest hit song, "Send in the Clowns." The show is a sophisticated, somewhat jaded look at a group of well-to-do Swedes at the turn of the century, among them a lawyer, Fredrik Egerman, his virginal child-bride, Anne, his former mistress, the actress Desirée Armfeldt, Desirée's current lover, the aristocratic Count Carl-Magnus Malcolm, the count's suicidal wife, other guests, and some witty servants. Eventually, the proper partners are sorted out during a weekend party at the country house of Desirée's mother, a former concubine of European nobility. A film version, with a change of locale to Vienna, was released in 1978. "The Glamorous Life," sung by Desirée's daughter, is an ensemble in the show; Sondheim adapted a solo version for the movie that appears in this volume.

MAME

MUSIC AND LYRICS: Jerry Herman
BOOK: Jerome Lawrence and Robert E. Lee
DIRECTOR: Gene Sachs
CHOREOGRAPHER: Onna White
OPENED: 5/24/66, New York; a run of 1,508 performances

Ten years after premiering the comedy based on Patrick Dennis' fictional account of his free-wheeling *Auntie Mame*, playwrights Lawrence and Lee joined forces with Jerry Herman to transform their play into a musical. Angela Lansbury, after years of stage and screen performances, finally achieved her stardom in the title role. In the story, Agnes Gooch, who is part of Mame's domestic staff, has been encouraged by the eccentric lady of the house to go out and *live*. In the late stages of pregnancy she returns to confront her mentor in "Gooch's Song." A 1983 revival, also starring Miss Lansbury, had a brief run on Broadway. A film version, virtually the last old-fashioned musical movie made, was released in 1974, starring Lucille Ball and Robert Preston, and from the original cast, Bea Arthur. The non-musical film of the story, *Auntie Mame*, was released in 1957 and starred Rosalind Russell.

ME AND JULIET

MUSIC: Richard Rodgers
LYRICS AND BOOK: Oscar Hammerstein II
DIRECTOR: George Abbott
CHOREOGRAPHER: Robert Alton
OPENED: 5/28/53, New York, a run of 358 performances

Me and Juliet was Rodgers and Hammerstein's valentine to show business, with its action—in *Kiss Me, Kate* fashion—taking place both backstage in a theatre and onstage during the performance of a play. Here the tale concerns a romance between a singer in the chorus and the assistant stage manager, whose newfound bliss is seriously threatened by the jealous electrician. A comic romantic subplot involves the stage manager and the principal dancer. Jeanie, the chorus girl ingenue in the musical, sings "A Very Special Day" backstage as the first number in the show, establishing her dreamy, romantic character.

THE MERRY WIDOW

MUSIC: Franz Lehár
BOOK AND LYRICS: Victor Léon and Leo Stein (the original in German)
OPENED: 1905, Vienna
1906, London (English lyrics by Adrian Ross); 778 performances
1907, New York; 416 performances

The epitome of the swirling, melodious, romantic post-Straussian Viennese operetta, *The Merry Widow* was first performed in Vienna as *Die lustige Witwe*. Its initial English-language version ran in London for 778 performances. This was the text that was used for the New York production, which was so acclaimed (a run of a year was an enormous hit in those days) that it even prompted the introduction of Merry Widow hats, gowns, corsets, and cigarettes. The story, based on a French play, *L'Attaché d'Ambassade*, is set in Paris and tells of the efforts of the ambassador of the imaginary kingdom of Marsovia to get his attaché, Prince Danilo, to marry the wealthy widow (named either Hanna or Sonya, depending on the version) so that she might contribute to the tiny country's dwindling finances. Though he balks at being a fortune hunter, Danilo finds himself falling in love and eventually proposes marriage—but only after the young widow has led him to believe that she is penniless. The operetta has had five Broadway revivals, the last and most successful in 1943 for a run of 322 performances, returning to New York after a tour to add another 32 performances. The piece has entered the regular repertories of many opera companies. There have been at least twelve different English versions of the show over the years, including a version by Broadway lyricist Sheldon Harnick.

THE MIKADO
or The Town of Titipu

MUSIC: Arthur Sullivan
LIBRETTO: W.S. Gilbert
OPENED: 3/14/1885, London

In the town of Titipu, the Lord High Executioner Ko-Ko prepares for his wedding. When his bride-to-be, Yum-Yum, arrives with her two sisters, she is met by Nanki-Poo, who also is in love with her. Word comes to Ko-Ko from the Mikado, the emperor of Japan, that it's been too long since anyone in Titipu has been executed; this must change! In truth, Ko-Ko is next in line for beheading, but he'd much rather find an alternate. Nanki-Poo, contemplating suicide rather than life without Yum-Yum, agrees to be executed instead, under the condition that he first be allowed a month as Yum-Yum's husband. As Yum-Yum prepares for the wedding, she marvels at her own beauty—not out of vanity, she says, but out of the frankness of nature ("The Sun, Whose Rays Are All Ablaze"). There are complications, of course: Nanki-Poo, who is not the wandering minstrel he pretends to be, but the Mikado's son, is pursued by the spinster Katisha, who would have him for her own. But in this lampoon of corruption in government, even underhanded officials can eventually bring about a happy ending.

THE MOST HAPPY FELLA

MUSIC, LYRICS AND BOOK: Frank Loesser
DIRECTOR: Joseph Anthony
CHOREOGRAPHER: Dania Krupska
OPENED: 5/3/56, New York; a run of 676 performances

Adapted from Sidney Howard's Pulitzer Prize-winning play, *They Knew What They Wanted*, Loesser's musical was a particularly ambitious work for the Broadway theatre, with more than thirty separate musical numbers, including arias, duets, trios, quartets, choral pieces, and recitatives. Robust, emotional expressions ("Joey, Joey, Joey" and "My Heart Is So Full of You") were interspersed with more traditional specialty numbers ("Big D" and "Standing on the Corner"), though in the manner of an opera; the program credits did not list individual selections. In the story, set in California's Napa Valley, an aging vineyard owner (originally played by opera singer Robert Weede) proposes by mail to a waitress he calls Rosabella. She accepts, but is so upset to find Tony old and fat that on their wedding night she allows herself to be seduced by Joe, the handsome ranch foreman. After some time, Rosabella learns to love Tony, to the point where he makes her feel "Warm All Over." However, she soon realizes Tony treats her not as an equal, but as a child. Her rhapsodic plea, "Like a Woman Loves a Man," changes his feelings toward his wife. Once Tony discovers that Rosabella is to have another man's child, he threatens to kill Joe, but there is a reconciliation and the vintner offers to raise the child as his own. A 1979 Broadway revival, starring Giorgio Tozzi, ran for 52 performances. A more successful revival ran in New York in 1991-2, resulting in a new recording of the score.

MY FAIR LADY

MUSIC: Frederick Loewe
LYRICS AND BOOK: Alan Jay Lerner
DIRECTOR: Moss Hart
CHOREOGRAPHER: Hanya Holm
OPENED: 3/15/56, New York; a run of 2,717 performances

The most celebrated musical of the 1950s began as an idea of Hungarian film producer Gabriel Pascal, who devoted the last two years of his life trying to find writers to adapt George Bernard Shaw's play, *Pygmalion*, into a stage musical. The team of Lerner and Loewe also saw the possibilities, particularly when they realized that they could use most of the original dialogue and simply expand the action. They were also scrupulous in maintaining the Shavian flavor in their songs. Shaw's concern with class distinction and his belief that barriers would fall if all Englishmen would learn to speak properly was conveyed through a story about Eliza Doolittle (a star-making role for Julie Andrews), a scruffy flower seller in London's Covent Garden, taken on as a speech student of linguistics Professor Henry Higgins (played by Rex Harrison) to increase her social and economic potential. Eliza succeeds so well that she outgrows her social station and even makes Higgins fall in love with her. Though the record was subsequently broken, *My Fair Lady* became the longest running production in Broadway history, remaining for over six and a half years. The show was also a solid success in London. For the 1964 movie version, Julie Andrews was passed over for Audrey Hepburn as Eliza (whose singing was dubbed by Marni Nixon), along with Harrison. Two major revivals have been mounted in New York as of this writing. In 1976 the musical ran for 377 performances with Ian Richardson and Christine Andreas. In 1981 New York again saw Rex Harrison in 119 performances with Nancy Ringham's Eliza. In the late 1980s a new recording of the musical was released with Kiri Te Kanawa and Jeremy Irons in the leading roles. "Without You" is Eliza's declaration of independence from her Svengali, Professor Higgins.

THE MYSTERY OF EDWIN DROOD

MUSIC, LYRICS AND BOOK: Rupert Holmes
DIRECTOR: Wilford Leach
CHOREOGRAPHER: Graciela Daniele
OPENED: 12/2/85, New York; a run of 608 performances

The Mystery of Edwin Drood came to Broadway after being intially presented the previous summer in a series of free performances sponsored by the New York Shakespeare Festival at the Delacorte Theatre in Central Park. The impressive score was the first stage work of composer-lyricist-librettist Rupert Holmes, who had previously revealed a talent limited to commercial pop. Holmes' lifelong fascination with Charles Dickens' unfinished novel had been the catalyst for the project. Since there were no clues as to Drood's murderer or even if a murder had been committed, Holmes decided to let the audience provide the show's ending by voting how it turns out. The writer's second major decision was to offer the musical as if it were being performed by an acting company at London's Music Hall Royale in 1873. On November 13, 1986, in an attempt to attract more theatre-goers, the musical's title was changed to *Drood*. "Moonfall" is Rosa's strange romantic song of longing, and "Rosa's Confession" is the song she sings if the audience votes for her as the killer.

NINE

MUSIC AND LYRICS: Maury Yeston
BOOK: Arthur Kopit, Mario Fratti
DIRECTOR: Tommy Tune
CHOREOGRAPHERS: Tommy Tune and Thommie Walsh
OPENED: 5/9/82, New York; a run of 732 performances

The influence of the director-choreographer was emphasized again with Tommy Tune's highly stylized, visually striking production of *Nine*, which, besides being a feast for the eyes is also one of the very few non-Sondheim Broadway scores to have true musical substance and merit from the 1970s and 1980s. The musical evolved from Yeston's fascination with Federico Fellini's semi-autobiographical 1963 film *8 1/2*. The story spotlights Guido Contini (played originally by Raul Julia), a celebrated but tormented director who has come to a Venetian spa for a rest, and his relationships with his wife, his mistress, his protégée, his producer and his mother. The production, which flashes back to Guido's youth and also takes place in his imagination, offers such inventive touches as an overture in which Guido conducts his women as if they were instruments, and an impressionistic version of the Folies Bergères. "A Call from the Vatican" refers to what Guido has told his secretary about a sexy phone call that comes from his mistress. "Unusual Way" is sung to Guido by his young actress protégée. "Simple" is sung by the mistress as Guido's midlife crisis accelerates, and he is temporarily left alone.

110 IN THE SHADE

MUSIC: Harvey Schmidt
LYRICS: Tom Jones
BOOK: N. Richard Nash
DIRECTOR: Joseph Anthony
CHOREOGRAPHER: Agnes de Mille
OPENED: 10/24/63, New York; 330 performances

N. Richard Nash adapted his own play, *The Rainmaker*, for Schmidt and Jones' first Broadway musical, following their wildly successful *The Fantasticks* Off Broadway. Nash's play is probably best remembered for the film version which starred Burt Lancaster and Katharine Hepburn. It is a simple tale of Lizzie, an aging, unmarried woman who lives with her father and brothers on a drought-stricken ranch in the American west. Starbuck, a transient "rainmaker," comes on the scene and is soon seen to be the con man that he is, despite his dazzling charisma. He does, however, pay somewhat sincere attention to Lizzie, and awakens love and life in her. Nevertheless, she sees no future with Starbuck, and winds up with a reliable local suitor instead. Inga Swenson was the musical's original Lizzie, with Robert Horton as Starbuck. The show was featured in a prominent production by New York City Opera in 1992. All Lizzie's songs show her conflicted character. In "Raunchy" she flirts with the idea, briefly, of becoming a brazen man-magnet. "Is It Really Me?" is sung to Starbuck after he has told her how beautiful she is. "Simple Little Things" reveals her true values, reflecting her no-nonsense rural American upbringing.

PHANTOM

MUSIC AND LYRICS: Maury Yeston
BOOK: Arthur Kopit

Though at this writing Yeston's *Phantom* has not had a Broadway run, it has played widely in the United States, receiving raves from critics in Chicago, Boston, New York, Dallas and other places. Based on the 1911 French novel, the show's principal characters are Christine and Phantom, and his protective love for her. Yeston and Kopit actually wrote their show before Lloyd Webber wrote his, but were unable to get any financing for a Broadway production after the new British musical was announced. *Phantom* was first seen in Houston in 1991. Among the show's strong score, "This Place Is Mine" is Carlotta's comic song about the opera house where she reigns. Yeston, composer of *Nine* and *Grand Hotel*, is certainly one of the most interesting composers to hit Broadway, with his background as a music textbook author and professor at Yale, and his compositional abilities, further represented by a cello concerto written for Yo-Yo Ma. He wrote the words and music for a song cycle called *December Songs*, commissioned for the Carnegie Hall centennial celebration. "My True Love" is Christine's song to the Phantom, asking to see his hidden face.

PHILEMON

MUSIC: Harvey Schmidt
WORDS: Tom Jones
OPENED: 1970, New York

The 60s had *The Fantasticks*, *110 in the Shade*, *I Do! I Do!*, and *Celebration* from Schmidt and Jones. Following those shows, the pair developed their own theatre workshop in New York called Portfolio, and in the spirit of that time concentrated on small scale, experimental musicals. *Philemon* was the most notable show to come out of the workshop, and won the Outer Critics Circle Award. "The Greatest of These" is based on the biblical text from 1 Corinthians, Chapter 13.

THE PIRATES OF PENZANCE

MUSIC: Arthur Sullivan
LIBRETTO: W.S. Gilbert
OPENED: 12/31/1879, New York

Twenty-one-year-old Frederic, bound by his sense of duty to serve out his apprenticeship to a band of pirates, has reached the end of his indentures and decides henceforth to oppose the cutthroat crew rather than join them. His nursemaid, Ruth who has served with him aboard ship as a maid-of-all-work, confesses that the whole thing had been a mistake from the beginning. After leaving the pirates, Frederic happens upon a party of young women—the daughters of the Major-General Stanley—one of whom, Mabel, takes pity on him ("Poor Wand'ring One"). The pirates then arrive on the scene, determined to marry the young ladies, but the Major-General wins clemency by claiming to be an orphan. Frederic, at first duty-bound to destroy his former comrades, rejoins them when he finds that his apprenticeship extends to his twenty-first birthday, and having been born on February 29, he has so far had only five birthdays. But in the end, the pirates yield to the police at the invocation of Queen Victoria's name, and when Ruth reveals that they are actually wayward noblemen, they earn their pardon and permission to marry the Major-General's daughters.

PLAIN AND FANCY

MUSIC: Albert Hague
LYRICS: Arnold B. Horwitt
BOOK: Joseph Stein and Will Glickman
DIRECTOR: Morton Da Costa
CHOREOGRAPHER: Helen Tamiris
OPENED: 1/27/55, New York; a run of 461 performances

The setting of *Plain and Fancy* was Amish country in Pennsylvania, where two worldly New Yorkers (Richard Derr and Shirl Conway) have gone to sell a farm they inherited—but not before they had a chance to meet the God-fearing people and appreciate their simple but unyielding way of living. The warm and atmospheric score, with its hit song "Young and Foolish" was composed by Albert Hague, familiar to television viewers as the bearded music teacher in the series "Fame." *Plain and Fancy* was another Barbara Cook show that helped to establish her as Broadway's favorite golden-throated ingenue.

REGINA

WORDS AND MUSIC: Marc Blitzstein
DIRECTOR: Robert Lewis
OPENED: 10/31/49, New York; a run of 56 performances

Regina is among the most distinguished and thrilling American scores for the stage, and in a style that combines a theatrical popularity and serious composition. Gershwin had tried opera on Broadway in 1935 with *Porgy and Bess*—the idea was ahead of its time, but had a great effect on composers to come. By the late 1940s to the early 1950s, there was a small but important trend toward a more grown-up, musically ambitious, serious lyric theatre for Broadway, with Gian Carlo Menotti, Kurt Weill, Marc Blitzstein the prime contributors. *Regina* is based on the Lillian Hellman 1939 play *The Little Foxes* (released as a film with Bette Davis in the title role). "What Will It Be for Me?" is the song of Regina's seventeen-year-old daughter, Alexandra, a good natured, innocent girl whose character is in sharp contrast to her mother.

THE SECRET GARDEN

MUSIC: Lucy Simon
LYRICS AND BOOK: Marsha Norman
DIRECTOR: Susan H. Schulman
CHOREOGRAPHER: Michael Lichtefeld
OPENED: 4/25/91, New York; 706 performances

Based on the novel by Frances Hodgson Burnett, the story is of an orphaned Mary Lennox, who is sent to live with her uncle Archibald in Yorkshire. He is absorbed in grief over the death of his young wife ten years earlier, and the house is gloomy and mysterious. Mary finds her dead aunt's "secret garden," passionately nurtures it to life, and Archie also comes back to life once he can let go of his grief. "How Could I Ever Know?" is sung by the ghost of his dead wife, Lilly.

SHE LOVES ME

MUSIC: Jerry Bock
LYRICS: Sheldon Harnick
BOOK: Joe Masteroff
DIRECTOR: Harold Prince
CHOREOGRAPHER: Carol Haney
OPENED: 4/23/63, New York; a run of 301 performances

The closely integrated, melody drenched score of *She Loves Me* is certainly one of the best ever written for a musical comedy. It was based on a Hungarian play, *Parfumerie*, by Miklos Laszlo, that had already been used as the basis for two films, *The Shop Around the Corner* and *In the Good Old Summertime* (with the setting changed to America). Set in the 1930s in Budapest, the tale is of the people who work in Maraczek's Parfumerie, principally the constantly squabbling sales clerk Amalia Balash (Barbara Cook) and the manager Georg Nowack (Daniel Massey). It is soon revealed that they are anonymous pen pals who agree to meet one night at the Café Imperiale, though neither knows the other's identity. Georg realizes that it is Amalia who is waiting for him in the restaurant, but doesn't let on, leaving her to sit there for hours, culminating in the pleaful "Dear Friend." After she calls in sick their relationship blossoms into love when Georg brings her ice cream; eventually, he is emboldened to reveal his identity by quoting from one of Amalia's letters. *She Loves Me*, which would have starred Julie Andrews had she not been filming *Mary Poppins*, was one of Barbara Cook's most magical portrayals. The show is well represented on the original cast album, which on two disks preserves practically every note of the show's music.

THE SOUND OF MUSIC

MUSIC: Richard Rodgers
LYRICS: Oscar Hammerstein II
BOOK: Howard Lindsay and Russel Crouse
DIRECTOR: Vincent J. Donehue
CHOREOGRAPHER: Joe Layton
OPENED: 11/16/59

Rodgers and Hammerstein's final collaboration became their third longest running Broadway production. The story of *The Sound of Music* was adapted from Maria Von Trapp's autobiographical *The Trapp Family Singers* and the German film version, which Mary Martin was convinced would provide her with an ideal stage vehicle. Her husband, Richard Halliday, and producer Leland Hayward secured the rights and, initially, they planned to use only the music associated with the famed singing family plus one additional song by Rodgers and Hammerstein. Eventually, the songwriters were asked to contribute the entire score, and they also joined Halliday and Hayward as producers.

The play is set in Austria in 1938. Maria Rainier (Miss Martin), a free-spirited postulant at Nonnburg Abbey, takes a position as governess to the seven children of the widowed and autocratic Capt. Georg Von Trapp (Theodore Bikel). After Maria and the captain fall in love and marry, their happiness is quickly shattered by the Nazi invasion which forces the family to flee over the Alps to Switzerland.

The 1965 film version, presented by 20th Century-Fox and directed by Robert Wise, starred Julie Andrews and Christopher Plummer. According to *Variety*, from 1966 through 1969 *The Sound of Music* was the All-Time Box-Office Champion in rentals received in the U.S.-Canadian market.

TWO BY TWO

MUSIC: Richard Rodgers
LYRICS: Martin Charnin
BOOK: Peter Stone
DIRECTOR: Joe Layton
OPENED: 1/10/70

After an absence of almost thirty years, Danny Kaye returned to Broadway in a musical based on the legend of Noah and the ark. Adapted from Clifford Odets' play, *The Flowering Peach*, *Two By Two* dealt primarily with Noah's rejuvenation and his relationship with his wife and family as he undertakes the formidable task that God has commanded. During the run, Kaye suffered a torn ligament in his left leg and was briefly hospitalized. He returned hobbling on a crutch with his leg in a cast, a situation he used as an excuse to depart from the script by cutting up and clowning around. For his third musical following Oscar Hammerstein's death, composer Richard Rodgers joined lyricist Martin Charnin (later to be responsible for *Annie*) to create a melodious score that included "I Do Not Know a Day I Did Not Love You."

SO FAR
from *Allegro*

Lyrics by OSCAR HAMMERSTEIN II
Music by RICHARD RODGERS

Refrain *(slowly, in four beats)*

We have noth-ing to re-mem-ber so far, so far,

So far we have-n't walked by night and shared the light of a star.

So far your heart has nev-er flut-tered so near, so near

That my own heart a-lone could

hear it. We have-n't gone be-

yond the ver-y be-gin-ning,——— We've just be-gun to

know how luck-y we are.——————— So

we have noth-ing to re-mem-ber so far, so

We haven't gone be - yond the ver - y be - gin - ning, We've just be - gun to know how luck - y we are So we have

ALL THROUGH THE NIGHT

from *Anything Goes*

Words and Music by
COLE PORTER

THE GYPSY IN ME

from *Anything Goes*

Words and Music by
COLE PORTER

Tip - sy no, no, _____ of their love there was - n't a doubt _____ So I can't

wait to get the stage all set, So I can let _____ the gyp - sy in me

(rit.)

[Moderato]

out. _____ Hid - ing a - way, _____

a tempo   stacc.

_____ There's a lit - tle bit of gyp - sy in _____ me _____ That's nev - er been

found. _____ Wait-ing its day _____

____ There's a lit-tle bit of gyp - sy in ___ me _____ Just hang-ing a - round,_

_____ Till the mag - i - cal night _____

____ When the stars by their light give mys - ter - y _____ to the sleep-ing la -

At the mo-ment su-preme _____

_____ will be shown the un-known gyp-sy in ___ me. _____

marc.

1

2

8vb ___

I'LL FOLLOW MY SECRET HEART

from *Conversation Piece*

Words and Music by
NOËL COWARD

You ask me to have a dis- creet heart Un-til mar-riage is out of the way, But what if I meet with a sweet-heart so sweet That my way-ward heart can-not o-

REFRAIN
(slow tempo di Valse)

I'll fol - low my se - cret heart my whole life through,_____ I'll keep all my dreams a - part till one comes true._____ No

TAKE ME TO THE WORLD

from *Evening Primrose*

Words and Music by
STEPHEN SONDHEIM

Moderato ma poco rubato (♩ = 80)

Let me see the world _____ with clouds, Take me to the world. _____

Out where I can push _____ through crowds, Take me to the world. _____ A

We shall have the world._____ I'll hold your hand And know I'm not a-lone. We shall have the world _____ to keep, Such a love-ly world _____ we'll weep. We shall have the world for - ev - er for our own._____

ART IS CALLING FOR ME

(The Prima Donna Song)
from *The Enchantress*

Music by VICTOR HERBERT
Lyrics by HARRY B. SMITH

Mam-ma is a queen, and pa-pa is a king; So
I'm in the é-lite, and men sigh at my feet; Still

I am a Prin-cess, I ___ know it; But
I do not fan-cy my po-si-tion; I

court et-i-quette is a dull drear-y thing, I just
have not much use for the men that I meet, I quite

op - 'ra by Sig - nor Puc - ci - ni. I've rou-
op - 'ra so charm - ing by Gou - nod. Girls would

poco meno *(tr)*

lades and the trills that would send the cold chills down the
be on the brink of hys - ter - ics, I think, e - ven

pesante *(tr)* *(ad lib.)*

backs of all hear - ers of my vo - cal frills. _____
strong men would have to go out for a drink. _____

colla voce

REFRAIN:

f

I long to be a pri - ma
I long to be a pri - ma

41

peach - y can - ta - *tri - ce, like oth - er **plump girls that I
"Vi - va" to the di - va, oh, ver - y love - ly that must

see; _____ I hate so -
be; _____ That's what I'm

ci - e - ty; I hate pro - pri - e - ty;
dy - ing for, That's what I'm sigh - ing for,

(D.C.)

Art is call - ing for me. _____
Art is call - ing for me. _____

* treechy
** optional lyric: "Songbirds" replacing "plump girls"

ANOTHER SUITCASE IN ANOTHER HALL

from *Evita*

Lyrics by TIM RICE
Music by ANDREW LLOYD WEBBER

It would be stylistically appropriate for the pianist to improvise an accompaniment.

**Sung as a chorus by other characters.*

time and time a-gain I've said that I don't care; That I'm im-mune to gloom, that I'm

hard ___ through and through: But ev-'ry time it mat-ters all my words de-sert me; So

an-y-one can hurt me and they do. So what hap-pens now? So what hap-pens

An-oth-er suit-case in an-oth-er hall. ___

I'LL KNOW
from *Guys and Dolls*

Lyrics and Music by
FRANK LOESSER

I'll know when my love comes a-long, I won't take a chance. For oh he'll be just what I need, not some fly - by-night Broad-way ro - mance. I'll know by the calm stead-y voice, those feet on the ground _____ I'll know as I

*Adapted as a solo here, the song is a
duet scene for Sarah and Sky in the show.*

(with mounting determination)

run to his arms that at last I've come home safe and sound and till then I shall

wait and till then I'll be strong for I'll know when my

love comes a - long.

I won't take a chance, my

love will be just what I need not some fly - by - night Broad - way ro -

mance, and till then I shall wait and till

then _____ I'll be strong _____ for I'll know when my

love _____ comes a - long. _____

IF I WERE A BELL
from *Guys and Dolls*

Words and Music by
FRANK LOESSER

Slowly *(Swing)*
Sarah: *(Very freely and slightly tipsy)*
(Spoken 1st vs.) ----------------- *(Sung)*

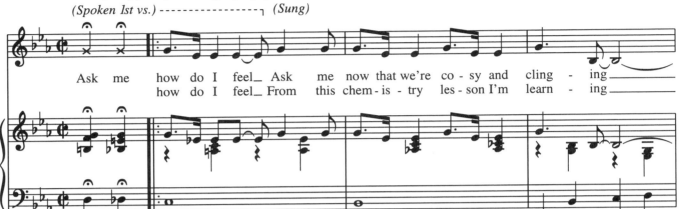

Ask me how do I feel_ Ask me now that we're co-sy and cling - ing_____
how do I feel_ From this chem-is-try les-son I'm learn - ing_____

Well, sir, all I can say ___ is, if I ___ were a bell ___ I'd be
Well, sir, all I can say ___ is, if I ___ were a bridge_ I'd be

ring - ing _____ From the mo-ment we kissed to-night_ That's the
burn - ing _____ Yes I knew my mo-rale would crack_ From the

AND THIS IS MY BELOVED

from *Kismet*

Music and Lyrics by
ROBERT WRIGHT and GEORGE FORREST
(based on themes of Alexander Borodin)

WHEN DID I FALL IN LOVE?

from *Fiorello!*

Lyrics by SHELDON HARNICK
Music by JERRY BOCK

THEA:
There he goes, my con-gress-man. Start-ing his

day hur-ry-ing right ___ to a fight. There he goes Sir

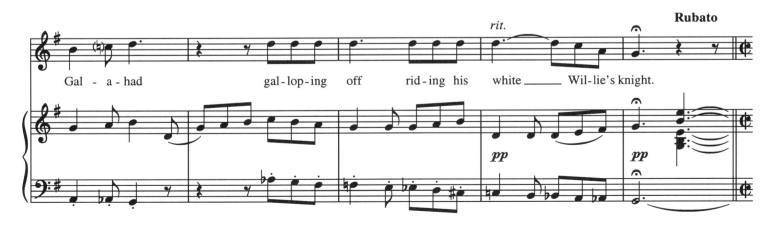

Gal-a-had gal-lop-ing off rid-ing his white ___ Wil-lie's knight.

Out of the house ten sec-onds and I miss him, _____ I miss him more with each good - bye. Out of the house ten sec-onds and I miss him, and no one's more as - ton-ished than I. I nev - er

Rubato

once pre - tend-ed that I loved him; _____ when did I start this change of

Slowly and tenderly

heart? _____ When did I fall in love? What night? Which day?

When did I first be - gin to feel this way? _____ How could the

mo - ment pass, un - felt, ig - nored? Where was the blind - ing flash?

Where was the crash - ing chord? When did I fall in love? I can't _____

sud-den-ly soar? _____ What a strange and beau-ti-ful touch

that I love him so much, when I did-n't be - fore. _____

When did I fall in love? Which night? Which day? When did I

first be - gin to feel this way? _____ How could the mo-ment pass, un-felt,

I LOVED

from *Jacques Brel Is Alive and Well and Living in Paris*

Original French Words by JACQUES BREL
English Words by MORT SCHUMAN and ERIC BLAU
Music by GÉRARD JOUANNEST and FRANÇOIS RAUBER

Poco meno mosso

I loved the towns where we made love, And the ho -

tels where we played games;

You thought I'd nev - er live it down, Yet you see, I've for - got - ten your name.

Più mosso

I WHISTLE A HAPPY TUNE

from *The King and I*

Lyrics by OSCAR HAMMERSTEIN II
Music by RICHARD RODGERS

[Moderato]

Oh _____ Oh, _____ When-ev-er I feel a-

fraid I hold my head e - rect And whis-tle a hap-py tune, So

no-one will sus - pect I'm a - fraid _____ While shiv-er-ing in my

shoes I strike a care-less pose And whis-tle a hap-py tune And no one ev-er knows I'm a-fraid _____ The re-sult of this de-cep-tion is ver-y strange to_ tell For when I fool the peo-ple I fear I fool my-self as well! I whis-tle a hap-py

Whistle

You may be as brave as you make be - lieve you

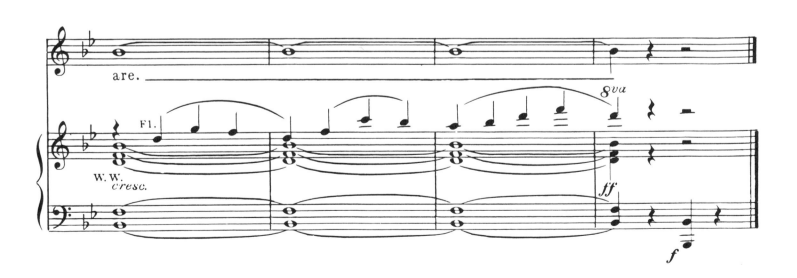

are.

I HATE MEN

from *Kiss Me, Kate*

Words and Music by
COLE PORTER

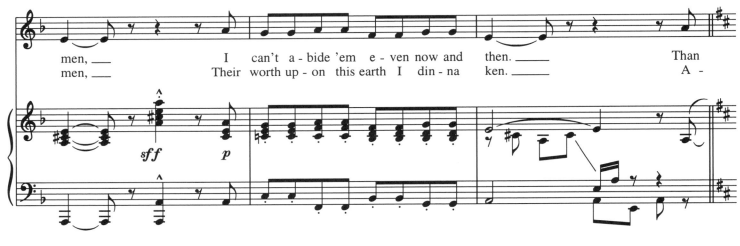

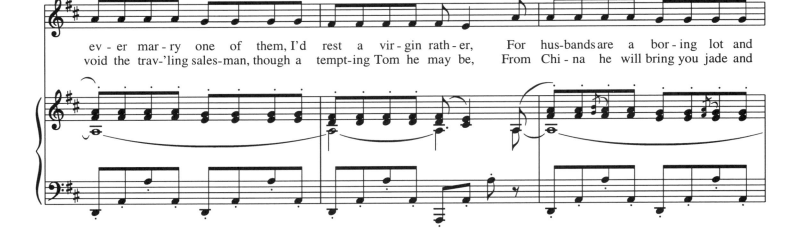

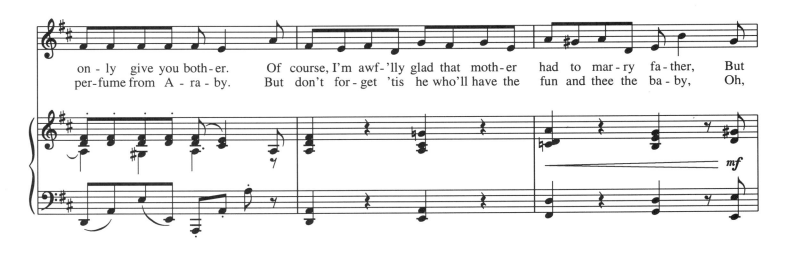

on - ly give you both - er. Of course, I'm awf-'lly glad that moth-er had to mar-ry fa-ther, But
per-fume from A - ra - by. But don't for-get 'tis he who'll have the fun and thee the ba-by, Oh,

cantabile   *gaily*

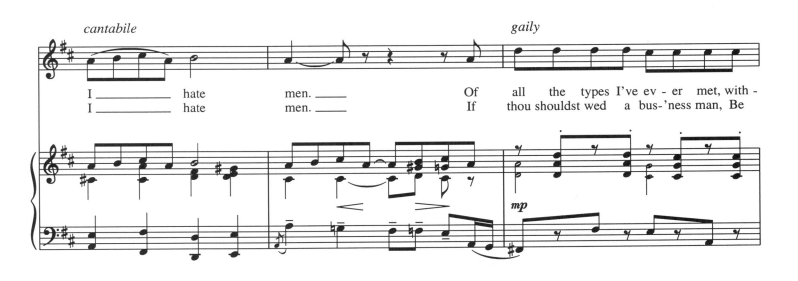

I _____ hate men. _____ Of all the types I've ev-er met, with -
I _____ hate men. _____ If thou shouldst wed a bus-'ness man, Be

in our de - mo - cra - cy, I hate the most, the ath - lete with his
wa - ry, oh be war - y, He'll tell you he's de - tained in town on

THE GLAMOROUS LIFE

from *A Little Night Music*

Music and Lyrics by
STEPHEN SONDHEIM

The song appears in a different form in the show.

Mend the clothes and tend the child-ren. Or - din-ar - y moth - ers, like

or - din-ar - y wives, Make the beds and

bake the pies and with - er on the vine. Not

tain - ing their poise.

Sand - wich - es on - ly, but she eats what she

wants when she wants.

Some - times it's lone - ly, _____ but she meets man - y

hand - some gal - lants.

Or - din - ar - y moth-ers don't live out of cas - es But

or - din - ar - y moth-ers don't go diff - 'rent pla - ces, Which

or - din - ar - y moth-ers can't do, Be - ing moth - ers all

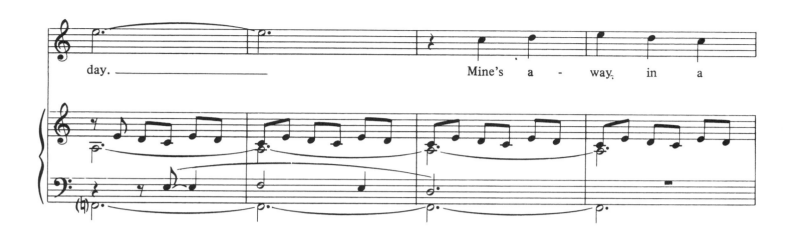

day. _____ Mine's a - way, in a

play _____ And she's real - er than

they. _____

L'istesso tempo

What if her broach is Only glass And her costumes un - rav - el? What if her coach is sec - ond class? She at least gets to trav - el.

cresc.

The Glamorous Life: 8-17

ov - er the green.

Some - time this sum - mer, _____ to the res - cue, my

mf

moth-er the queen! _____

f
Or - din - ar - y moth-ers thrive on be - ing pri - vate, And

f

LOOK FOR A SKY OF BLUE

from *Little Mary Sunshine*

Music and Lyrics by
RICK BESOYAN

GOOCH'S SONG

from *Mame*

Music and Lyric by
JERRY HERMAN

With my wings res-o-lute-ly spread, Mis-sis Burn-side, And my old in-hi-bi-tions shed, Mis-sis Burn-side, I did each lit-tle thing you said, Mis-sis Burn-side. I lived! I lived! I lived! I

Moderately slow 2

al - tered the drape of a drop of my bod - ice And

soft - ened the shape of my brow. I

fol - lowed di - rec - tions, And made some con - nec - tions, But

what do I do now? Who'd

think this Miss Prim would Have o - pened a win - dow As

far as her whim would al - low? _____ And

who would sup - pose it Was so hard to close it, Oh,

what do I do now? _____ I

thanks for the train-ing Now I'm not com-plain-ing, But

you left some-thing out!_____ In-stead of

wan-d'ring on with my lone re-morse, I have come back home to com-plete the course. Oh,

What do I do ---

thrived on your theo-ry That life can be a wow! _____

Freely

You said there's noth-ing wrong with a harm-less smooch, So I'm gon-na call him

Tempo I⁰

Burn-side Gooch! Oh, what do I do

now? _____

THE SUN, WHOSE RAYS ARE ALL ABLAZE

from *The Mikado*

Words by W.S. GILBERT
Music by ARTHUR SULLIVAN

As he the sky We real-ly know our worth, ___ The sun and I!

cresc.   *dim.*

rall.   *a tempo*

I mean to rule the earth, As he the sky We real-ly know our worth, The sun and I!

rall.   *a tempo*   *mf*

Ob-serve his flame, That plac-id dame, The moon's Ce - les - tial High - ness;

p sostenuto

There's not a trace Up-on her face Of dif-fi-dence or shy-ness: She bor-rows light That, thro' the night, Man-kind may

all ac - claim her! And, truth to tell, She lights up well; So I, for one, don't blame her.

Ah, pray make no mis - take, _____ We are not shy; We're

p *cresc.*

ver - y wide a - wake, _____ The moon and I! Ah, pray make no mis-take, We are not shy; We're

dim.

rall.

ver - y wide a-wake, The moon and I!

rall. *a tempo* *mf* *p*

A VERY SPECIAL DAY

from *Me and Juliet*

Lyrics by OSCAR HAMMERSTEIN II
Music by RICHARD RODGERS

Tranquillo

JEANIE:

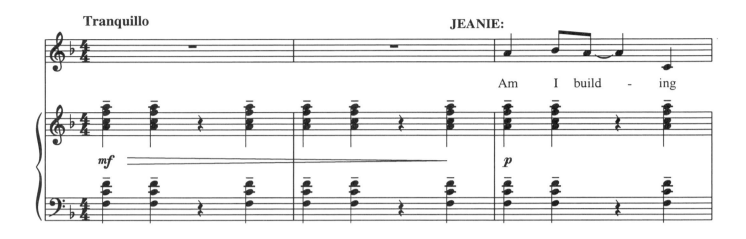

Am I build - ing

some - thing up ___ That real - ly is - n't there?

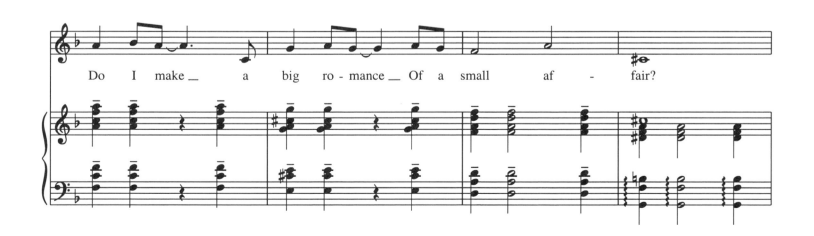

Do I make ___ a big ro - mance ___ Of a small af - fair?

I keep right on cling-ing To that feel-ing in my heart 'Til the

winds of eve-ning blow my dream a-way.

dolce

espr. Lat-er on at bed-time, When my world has come a-part And I'm

in my far from fan-cy neg-li-gee With a

VILIA
from *The Merry Widow*
(Die Lustige Witwe)

Words by VIKTOR LEON and LEO STEIN
English Version by MARTHA GERHART
Music by FRANZ LEHÁR

an?
why,
Bang fleht ein lieb - kran - ker Mann!
in your em - bra - ces, I die!

Vil - ja, o Vil - ja, was thust Du mir
Vi - lia, oh Vi - lia, will love tell me

(opt. 2nd time)

LIKE A WOMAN LOVES A MAN

from *The Most Happy Fella*

By FRANK LOESSER

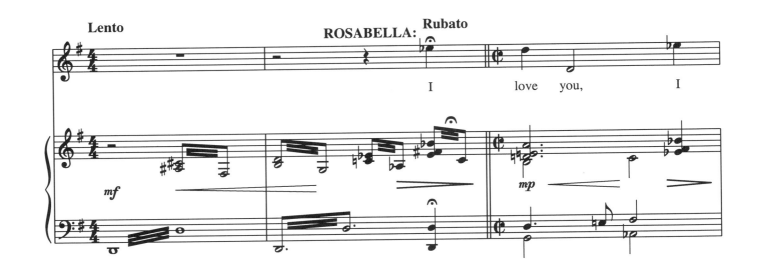

WARM ALL OVER
from *The Most Happy Fella*

Music and Lyrics by
FRANK LOESSER

clouds that used to swarm all o - ver. Please al - ways

let me keep feel - ing the way I do, so warm all

o - ver with a ten - der love for

you.

WITHOUT YOU

from *My Fair Lady*

Lyrics by ALAN JAY LERNER
Music by FREDERICK LOEWE

Allegro con anima

ELIZA:

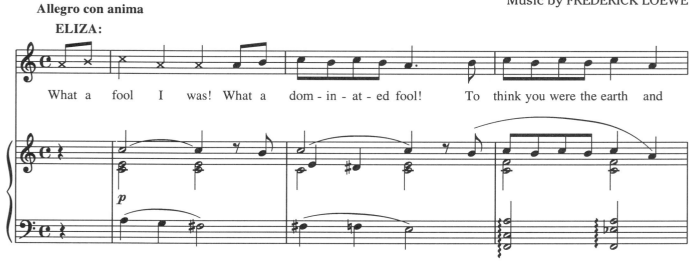

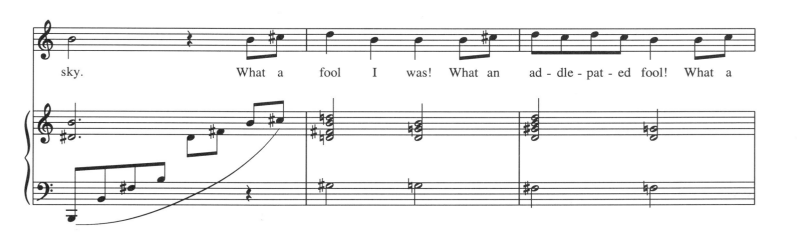

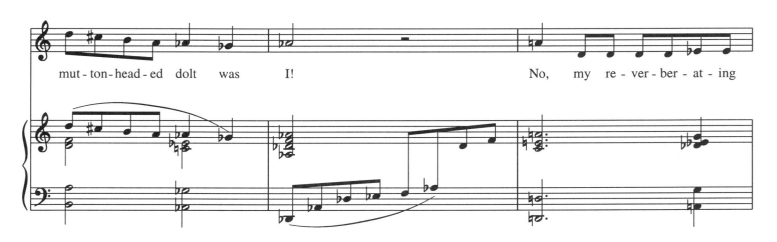

friend, You are not the be - gin - ning and the end! _____ There'll be

Allegro con moto

spring ev - 'ry year with-out you. Eng-land still will be here with-out

you. There'll be fruit on the tree; and a shore by the sea; there'll be

crum - pets and tea with - out you. Art and mu - sic will thrive with-out

you.　Some-how Keats will sur-vive with-out you.　And there

still will be rain on that plain down in Spain, e-ven that will re-main with-out

you.　I can do _____ with-out

you.　You, dear friend, who talk so

well, you can go to Hart - ford, Her - es - ford and

Hamp - shire. __ They can still rule the land with-out you. _____ Wind-sor Cas - tle will stand with-out

you. _____ And with - out much a - do we can all mud - dle through with-out

Poco meno

you. With - out your pull-ing it, the tide comes in; with -

out your twirl-ing it, the earth can spin. With-out your push-ing them, the clouds roll by. If

p   *sf*   *p*   *poco rall.*

Tempo giusto   **Tempo I**

they can do with-out you, duck-y,   so can I! I shall   not   feel a-lone   with-out

sf   *p*

you.   I can stand   on my own   with-out   you. _____ So go

f   *p*

back in your shell, I can do blood-y well with-out you! _____

f

MOONFALL
from *The Mystery of Edwin Drood*

Words and Music by
RUPERT HOLMES

Andante, molto espressivo

Be-tween the ver - y dead of night and day, up - on a steel - y sheet of light, I'll lay, and in the moon - fall, _____ I'll give my - self to you. _____ I'll bathe in moon - fall _____ and dress my - self in dew.

(Tempo-less, ad lib.)

Be - fore the cloak of night re - veals the morn,

time holds its dream while it con - ceals the dawn, and in the moon - fall, ___ all sound is

fro - zen still. ___ Yet warm a - gainst me, ___ your skin will warm the chill of

moon - fall. ___ I feel its fin - gers; lin - gers ___ the veil of

night - shade, light made from stars that all - too - soon fall,

moon - fall _____ that pours from you.   Be - twixt our hearts, let noth - ing

in - ter - vene.   Be - tween our eyes, the on - ly sight   I've seen

is lus - trous moon - fall as it blinds   my view,   so that soon I on - ly see but

you. _____

ROSA'S CONFESSION

from *The Mystery of Edwin Drood*

Words and Music by
RUPERT HOLMES

Were you so blind you could not see I killed him? Yes! And it was won-der-ful to do, I do con-fess. To have it done, to do him in, to see it through... You surely know by now I meant to mur-der you!

Thought you I was so blind as not to know your mind, of what in-tent each com-pli-ment you claimed you meant as kind? To feel my-self un-robed and probed with ev-'ry move-ment of your eyes? Ah, but re-al-ize: a child can go quite mad and not know good from bad and

calm - ly plan to kill a man and feel but on - ly glad! To rid her-self— to bid her-self a

mur - der - ous good - bye! Not Ed - win who I sought, but *you*, I

fp *fp* *subito p*

meant for *you* to die!

f *ff*

But the night was far from bright, thick with wet and thun - der. Thatch-ing fell dis-patched from hell!

Is it yet a won - der? Could not see the arms of me stretched out with scarf in hand.

Saw your coat and tied Ned's throat just like a dead - ly wed - ding band!

cresc. *sfz* *p*

Faster

So long a time they've thought that I'm a Dres - den

sfz *p* *f* *p*

doll, quite na - ive. But I be - lieve this pain, my brain more

tor - tured than they might con - ceive. With these late ad - di - tions, I have now re - vealed

mur - der - ous ad - mis - sions hith - er - to con - cealed. Damn you all, I say! You

let him drive me mad! Mad - ness led to this, no good can come from bad, no

good — no good can come from bad!! _____

A CALL FROM THE VATICAN

from *Nine*

Lyrics and Music by
MAURY YESTON

Note: Most of this song is belted.

UNUSUAL WAY
(IN A VERY UNUSUAL WAY)
from *Nine*

Lyrics and Music by
MAURY YESTON

SIMPLE
from *Nine*

Lyrics and Music by
MAURY YESTON

RAUNCHY
from *110 in the Shade*

Lyrics by TOM JONES
Music by HARVEY SCHMIDT

pour per - ox - ide on __ my head. __ I'll knock those poor old

Spoken:

cow - boys dead. You don't be - lieve me? __ Well, just watch! __

Blues tempo, in 4

I'll be so raunch - y, danc - in' in my pink and green sa -

teen. Feel - in' like a queen. __

Shak - in' my ca - boose. __ I'll be so raunch - y,

Step-pin' in my pat - ent leath - er shoes. __ *(Spoken)* When the

cow - boys see me strut __ my stuff, __ gon - na crawl right on their

haunch - es, 'cause they just can't seem to get __ e - nough, __ I'm a

raunch - y kind of gal. I'll be so raunch - y, when I'm danc - in'

up and down the street, of the coun - ty seat. __

Tip - py tap - pin' feet. __ I'll be so raunch - y,

All the fel - la's think I'm might - y sweet. When the

IS IT REALLY ME?

from *110 in the Shade*

Lyrics by TOM JONES
Music by HARVEY SCHMIDT

see.

Some-one who is _____ beau-ti-ful;

Is it real - ly me?

Mo-ments a - go,

I was a-lone hop-ing that this could be.

Now here I am, safe in your arms.

And I'm no long - er lone - ly.

SIMPLE LITTLE THINGS

from *110 in the Shade*

Lyrics by TOM JONES
Music by HARVEY SCHMIDT

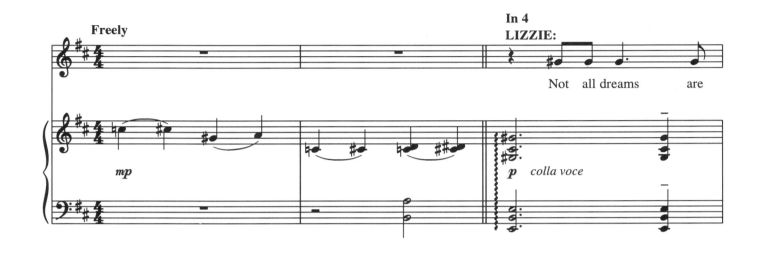

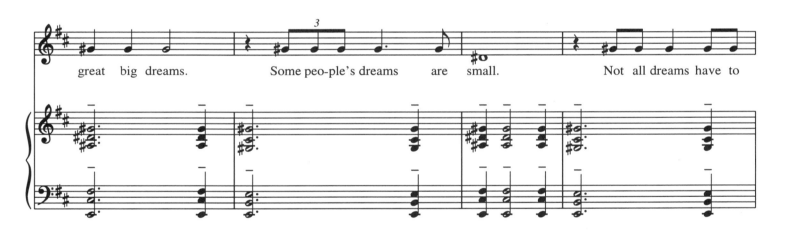

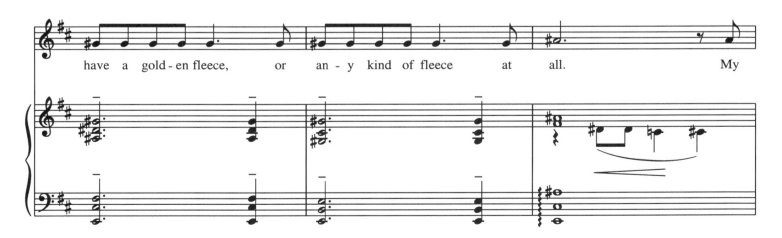

dreams, like my name, are ver-y plain; no shin-ing knight must kneel. My

dreams, like my name, are ver-y plain; but nev-er-the-less, they're

real. They're all so ver-y real.

poco rall.

Sim-ple lit-tle dreams, will do.

"Liz-zie, __ is my blue suit pressed?

Liz-zie, __ kind-a' scratch be-tween my shoul-der blades.

Liz-zie, __ are the

chil-dren all in bed?" That's what he'll say, I'll say: "My hus-band."

poco rall.

pp

rit.

THIS PLACE IS MINE

from *Phantom*

Words and Music by
MAURY YESTON

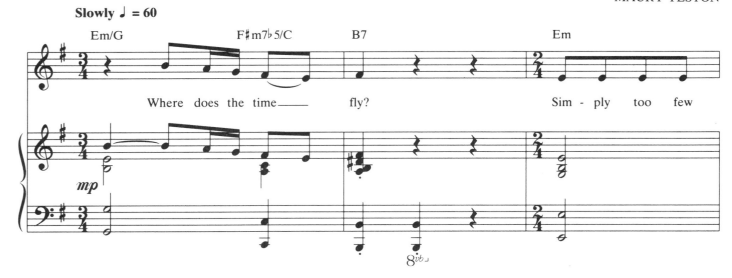

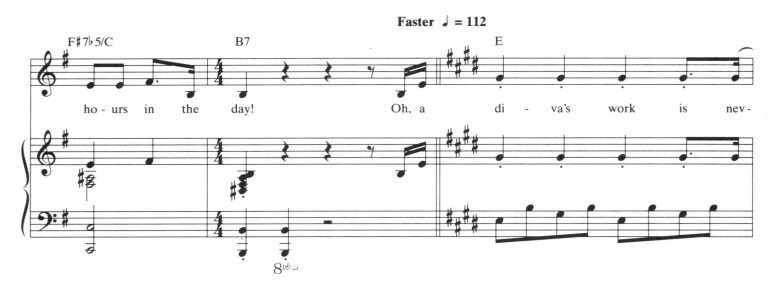

MY TRUE LOVE

from *Phantom*

Words and Music by
MAURY YESTON

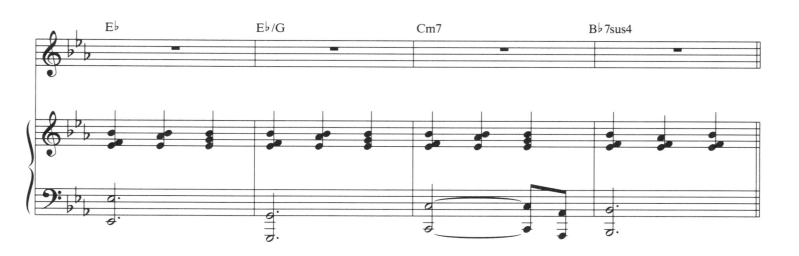

My   true   love,   lost   in   a
No,   my   love,   more   than   a

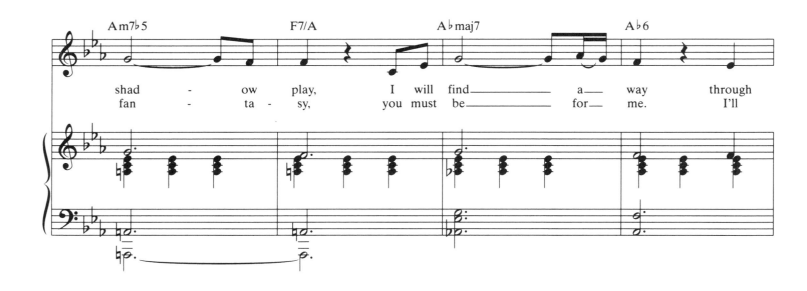

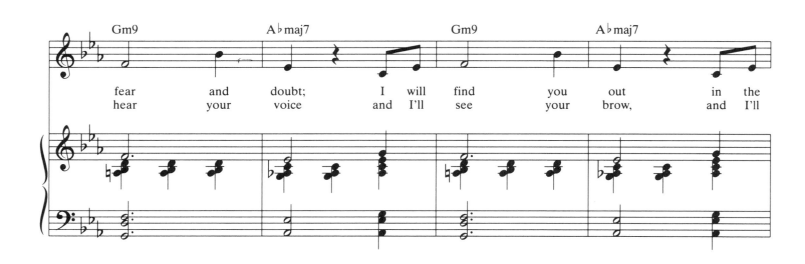

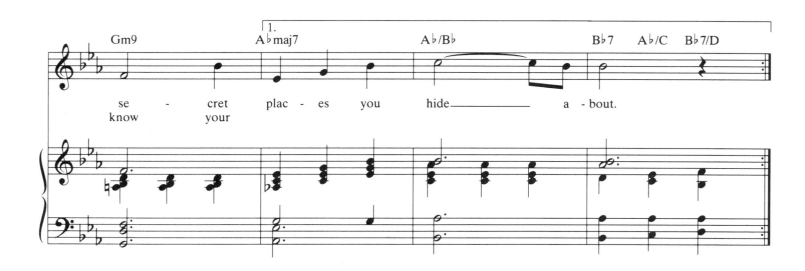

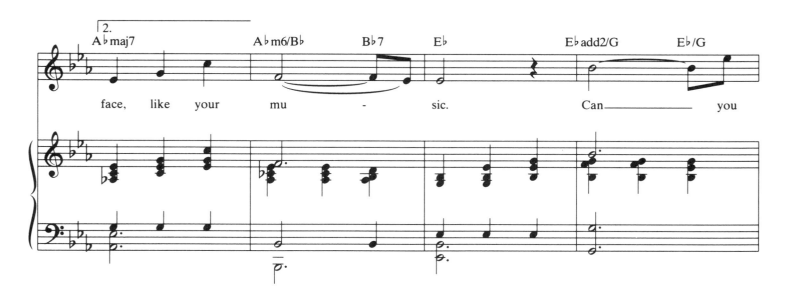

face, like your mu - sic. Can_____ you

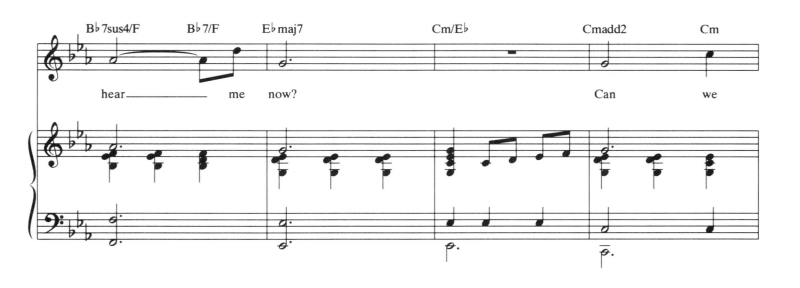

hear_____ me now? Can we

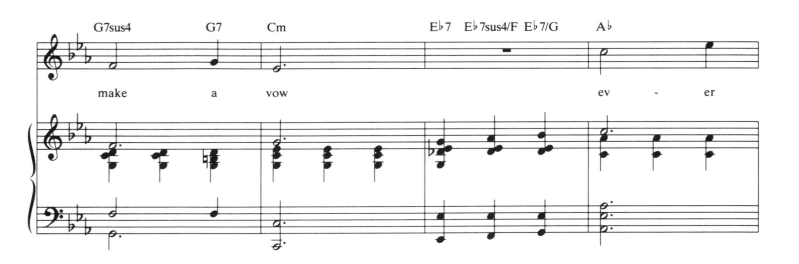

make a vow ev - er

THE GREATEST OF THESE

from *Philemon*

Lyrics by TOM JONES
Music by HARVEY SCHMIDT

Simply (♩ = 104)

Though I speak with the tongues of men and an - gels and have not love, and have not love; Though I'm blessed with the spe - cial gift of proph - e-cy, and have not love, and have not

love; Though my faith is strong e - nough to move a

moun - tain. Though I be - stow my world - ly goods to feed the

poor. Though my bod - y may be tor - tured, if I

have not lived with love I am noth-ing but a sound-ing brass a tin-kling cym-bal,

noth-ing, noth-ing. But with love, I can bear it all re-

joic - ing, be - cause of love be - cause of

love. _____ For love suf - fers ev - 'ry-thing

love bear - eth ev - 'ry-thing! Love hop - eth ev - 'ry-thing!

Broader

Love be-liev - eth ev - 'ry-thing! There a - bid - eth three things:

8va

ff   *mf*   *mp*

Faith, hope and love.   But the great - est of these   is

p   *pp*   *rit.*

opt. ending

love   My dear-est hus - band   what - e - ver they do   Don't let them

p *a tempo*   *mp*

take a - way your a - bil - i - ty to love.

rit.   *a tempo*

rit.   *decresc. e molto rit.*

POOR WAND'RING ONE
from *The Pirates of Penzance*

Words by W.S. GILBERT
Music by ARTHUR SULLIVAN

Take mine!

f a tempo

Ah! ah! _____ Ah. _____

_____ Take heart.

ff

Ped.

IT WONDERS ME

from *Plain and Fancy*

Lyrics by ARNOLD B. HORWITT
Music by ALBERT HAGUE

day can be, _____ So green the field, _____ So blue the sky, _____

_____ So red and gold _____ the map - le tree. _____

Some-where a breeze _____ be - gins to sing _____ Some-where a bird _____

_____ is an - swer-ing, _____ So won-der-ful sweet _____ the

So green the field, _____ So blue the sky, _____

_____ So red and gold _____ the ma - ple tree, _____

_____ Some-where a breeze _____ be - gins to sing _____

_____ Some-where a bird _____ is an - swer - ing, _____

WHAT WILL IT BE FOR ME?

from *Regina*

Words and Music by
MARC BLITZSTEIN

Who'll stand out-side, and wait, And won-der will I o-pen?

cresc. e rit. *f* *a tempo*

O - pen to what daz - zling light? _____ My life is

dim.

wait - ing _____ for me. _____ I won-der what will ____

rit. *mp* *a tempo* *rit.*

it be? _____

8va - - - - - - - - -

rit. *p* *a tempo* *rit.* *pp*

HOW COULD I EVER KNOW?

from *The Secret Garden*

Lyrics by MARSHA NORMAN
Music by LUCY SIMON

I DON'T KNOW HIS NAME

from *She Loves Me*

Lyrics by SHELDON HARNICK
Music by JERRY BOCK

mu - sic there. A home, a life, that's warm and full and rich in love and

art. _____ I don't need to see his hand-some pro - file. I don't need to

see his man-ly frame. All I need to know is in each let - ter. Each long re - veal-ing

let-ter. I could-n't know him bet - ter if I knew his name.

WILL HE LIKE ME?

from She Loves Me

Lyrics by SHELDON HARNICK
Music by JERRY BOCK

does-n't will he know e-nough to know _____ That there's more to me than I may al-ways

show? Will he like me? Will he know that there's a

With more motion

world of love wait-ing to warm him? How I'm hop-ing that his

eyes and ears won't mis-in-form him. Will he like me, who can

Broaden

pen. _____ Will he know that there's a world of love

wait - ing to warm him? How I'm hop - ing that his eyes and

ears won't mis - in - form him. Will he like me? I don't

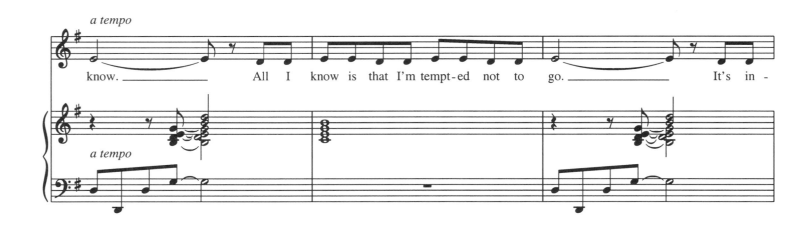

know. _____ All I know is that I'm tempt-ed not to go. _____ It's in -

DEAR FRIEND

from *She Loves Me*

Lyrics by SHELDON HARNICK
Music by JERRY BOCK

Poignantly (slowly)

pp

AMALIA:

Charm - ing, ro - man - tic, the per - fect ca - fé.

Then as if it is - n't bad e - nough, a vi - o - lin starts to play.

Can - dles and wine, ta - bles for two,

but where are you, dear friend?

cou - ples go past me, I see how they look.

So dis-creet-ly sym-pa - thet - ic when they see the rose and the book.

I make be - lieve, noth - ing is wrong.

212

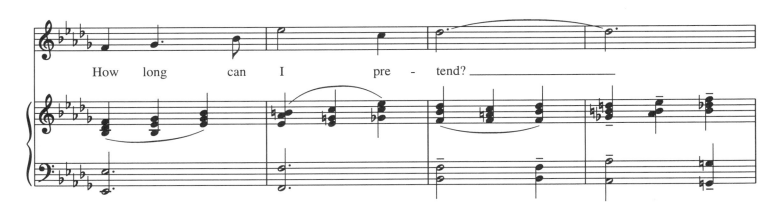

How long can I pre - tend? _____

please make it right. don't break my heart.

Don't let it end, dear friend.

I DO NOT KNOW A DAY
I DID NOT LOVE YOU

from *Two by Two*

Lyrics by MARTIN CHARNIN
Music by RICHARD RODGERS

Japheth sings the song in Act I; Rachel sings a reprise in Act II.

har - vest when the sun danced in your hair. _____

_____ I do not know a day I did not

need you, _____ For shar - ing ev - 'ry

ten.

mo - ment that I spent. _____ I

fact a - lone is full (and filled with song).

You will not know a day I do not

love you The way that I have loved you

all a - long.

THE SOUND OF MUSIC

from *The Sound of Music*

Lyrics by OSCAR HAMMERSTEIN II
Music by RICHARD RODGERS

Allegretto animato (♩ = 144)

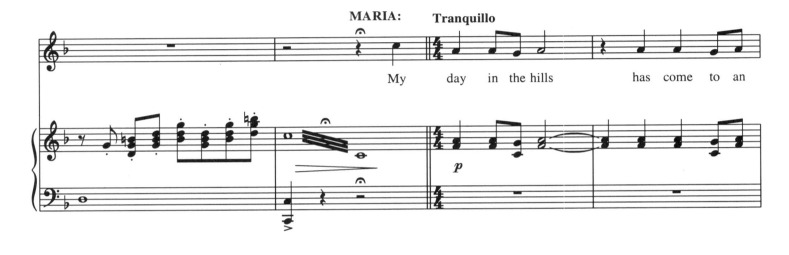

MARIA: Tranquillo

My day in the hills has come to an

end, I know. A star has come out to tell me it's

time to go. But deep in the dark green shad - ows are